NCE QUEST

The Search for

Forensic Evidence

Please visit our web site at: www.garethstevens.com
For a free color catalog describing Gareth Stevens Publishing's list of high-quality books
and multimedia programs, call 1-800-542-2595 (USA) or 1-800-387-3178 (Canada).
Gareth Stevens Publishing's fax: (414) 332-3567.

Library of Congress Cataloging-in-Publication Data

Innes, Brian.
    The search for forensic evidence / by Brian Innes. — North American ed.
      p. cm. — (Science quest)
    Includes index.
    ISBN 0-8368-4556-0 (lib. bdg.)
    1. Criminal investigation—Juvenile literature. 2. Crime scene searches—Juvenile literature.
    3. Forensic sciences—Juvenile literature. 4. Evidence, Criminal—Juvenile literature. I. Title. II. Series.
    HV8073.8.I55   2005
    363.25—dc22   2004059000

This North American edition first published in 2005 by
Gareth Stevens Publishing
A WRC Media Company
330 West Olive Street, Suite 100
Milwaukee, WI 53212 USA

This edition copyright © 2005 by Gareth Stevens, Inc. Original edition copyright © 2004 by ticktock Entertainment Ltd.,
First published in Great Britain in 2004 by ticktock Media Ltd., Unit 2, Orchard Business Centre, North Farm Road, Tunbridge Wells,
Kent, TN2 3 XF. Additional end matter copyright 2005 by Gareth Stevens, Inc.

Gareth Stevens editor: Jim Mezzanotte
Gareth Stevens designer: Kami M. Koenig

Photo Credits: (t=top, b=bottom, c=center, l=left, r=right)
Alamy: 14, 15 (t). Corbis: title page, 4-5 (c), 5 (t), 10 (c), 15 (b), 18, 25 (t), 25 (b), 26 (all), 27 (all). Getty Images: 8, 22, 28
(all), 29. Reuters: 5 (b), 7 (b). Rex Features: 6(b), 11, 20, 21 (b), 23(br), 24. Science Photo Library: 2-3, 7 (t), 9(c), 9 (b), 10
(b), 12 (all), 16 (all), 17, 19, 21 (t).

Printed in the United States of America

1 2 3 4 5 6 7 8 9 09 08 07 06 05

Contents

Words that appear in the glossary are printed in
boldface type the first time they occur in the text.

The word forensic means "having to do with a court of law." It describes any expert testimony about a crime that is given in court at a criminal trial. There are two kinds of criminal evidence. One kind involves descriptions given by witnesses, police investigators, and others associated with the criminal act itself. The other kind involves physical evidence at the scene of the crime. Forensic scientists analyze this kind of evidence to learn more about a crime.

Crime and Science

Criminal acts include **burglary**, various forms of theft, **fraud**, **extortion**, **arson**, physical assault, kidnapping, and murder. All of these crimes may require analysis of evidence by forensic scientists. Without the help of forensic science, it is likely that thousands of crimes would remain unsolved or even undetected. The scientific examination of crime has only developed in the last two hundred years, but now there are specialists in every field of forensic investigation. The victim of a violent act, whether dead or alive, is often examined by a medical expert. A victim who has died will be studied by a **medical examiner**, who practices **forensic pathology**. What the examiner discovers may then be further investigated by one or more experts in other fields of science.

Forensic scientists examine human tissue and bone to find clues that might help solve a crime.

Many Specialists

Some forensic scientists specialize in detecting and identifying fingerprints, while other experts, called **serologists**, investigate blood and other body fluids found at a crime scene. **Ballistics** experts study guns and bullets used in a crime. **Biologists** identify seeds and other plant and animal **traces** at a crime scene. They can tell how long a dead body has lain undiscovered, for example, by the different species of insects that have fed upon it. Other scientists keep records of paint and glass **samples**, hairs and fibers, and different kinds of tires and other manufactured products. If a pathologist's report suggests a victim has been poisoned, **toxicologists** are called in to find out how. In cases in which bones are all that remain of a murder victim, **anthropologists** can tell the age, sex, height, and even race of the victim by studying those bones. Handwriting experts can show who was responsible for a written message, while **psychologists** can examine the scene of a crime and establish a profile of the person who may have committed it.

Forensic scientists rush to the scene of a serious crime before vital evidence, which might help solve the case, is disturbed.

*When police are called to the scene of a serious crime, the area is immediately cordoned off from the general public in order to prevent **contamination** of vital evidence.*

5

About one hundred years ago, a French scientist, Dr. Edmond Locard, defined the first rule of criminal investigation: "Every contact leaves a trace." Dr. Locard was referring to the fact that most criminals leave behind evidence of their criminal actions. At crime scenes, forensic scientists search for this evidence.

Protecting the Crime Scene

After a crime has been committed, the crime scene has to be protected so evidence is not disturbed. Police officers usually seal off a crime scene by running tape around it. A forensic team may then arrive. This team will make sure that every piece of evidence, no matter how tiny, is found and preserved. The team must be careful not to contaminate the scene by introducing outside substances to it. To prevent such contamination, team members usually wear disposable gloves and disposable coverings for pants and shoes, all of which are extremely clean.

Searching for Clues

Once a crime scene has been sealed, a team slowly and carefully searches the site for anything that would not normally be there. The team puts every potential piece of evidence into a separate bag or box, with a note of exactly where it was collected. The container is sealed and initialed by one or more officers. It goes to an evidence room at the police station, then to a forensic expert for examination and analysis. Evidence found at the scene of a crime might include a fingerprint, a hair, some fibers from a sweater, or a footprint. It might also be a bullet, a cigarette end, or a written note.

SCIENCE CONCEPTS

Evidence found at a crime scene must immediately be bagged to prevent contamination.

The Chain of Custody

After evidence is found at a crime scene, a record must be kept of every person who handles it. The evidence may be needed in the courtroom at trial. If there is any doubt about who handled the evidence, it will not be considered credible. During the trial of former football star O. J. Simpson, who was **acquitted** of murdering two people, his **defense** argued that blood samples from the crime scene may have been improperly handled.

This scanning electron micrograph (SEM) shows pink **algae** particles, called diatoms, found on the clothing of a suspected burglar. Diatoms can help to establish a relationship between a suspect, victim, and crime scene.

Forensic officials often wear disposable clothing to avoid contaminating vital evidence recovered from a crime scene.

What a criminal takes away could be spots of blood from a victim who was attacked or a scratch on the face from a victim who fought back. It could also include mud or sand from the scene that became stuck in the sole of a shoe or in a car tire, something stolen, or fragments of the victim's clothing. Anything found could become the most important piece of evidence in solving a crime.

SCIENCE SNAPSHOT

Even the tiniest speck of dust might become the clue that helps to solve a crime. When a forensic team searches an indoor crime scene, they may use a small, handheld vacuum cleaner. This vacuum cleaner can suck up trace evidence from cracks in the floorboards and around the edges of a room.

Fingerprint Facts

Fingerprints are one of the most important pieces of evidence in a crime. They can prove that a suspect was present at a crime scene, and they can also help to identify an unknown dead person. A fingerprint provides reliable identification because no two people — not even twins — have the same fingerprints.

We Are All Unique

The patterns of lines on our fingertips, palms, and soles of our feet begin to form about five months before we are born, and they remain the same throughout our lives. One of the first people to discover this fact was a Scottish doctor, Henry Faulds, working in a Japanese hospital 130 years ago. Faulds and his students tried all kinds of ways to make their fingertips smooth, but every time, the same patterns grew back. At about the same time, William Herschel, an English **magistrate** in India who was working on a fraud case, noticed that fingerprints could be used to distinguish one person from another and help prevent fraud. About thirty years later, in 1901, London's Scotland Yard created a system for describing individual fingerprints. Today, many police forces have special departments for fingerprint analysis.

SCIENCE CONCEPTS

a) Radial loop   b) Ulnar loop   c) Plain arch   d) Tented arch

e) Plain whorl   f) Central pocket whorl   g) Double loop   h) accidental

Classifying Fingerprints

In 1901, British policeman Sir Edward Henry introduced the basic method for classifying fingerprint patterns. At left are eight typical patterns: radial loop (a), ulnar loop (b), plain arch (c), tented arch (d), plain whorl (e), central pocket whorl (f), double loop (g), and accidental (h).

Fingerprint Methods

Our fingers leave behind prints in minute traces of sweat. The standard method for finding fingerprints is to use a fine powder, blown or brushed across surfaces, that will stick to this sweat to reveal prints. In recent years, other methods have been created. One method uses fumes from glue to reveal prints. Another method finds prints with laser light. Various chemical sprays can also be used.

Collecting Fingerprints

When police arrest a crime suspect, they take the suspect's fingerprints. All ten fingers are covered with ink and pressed on a card. Today, some police forces use computers instead of an ink impression on a card. Each finger is scanned and then registered directly into a computer database. Using computers can greatly reduce the amount of time needed to take fingerprints of suspects.

Fingerprints can be revealed by dusting a surface with a fine powder. In this photo, fine iron particles reveal prints on a plastic tile. A magnet is used to remove excess particles from the surrounding area.

SCIENCE SNAPSHOT

When forensic scientists examine outdoor crime scenes, they often look for tracks left behind by tires. These tracks can be as important as fingerprints. Forensic scientists take casts and photographs of tire tracks at a crime scene and try to match these tracks to the tread patterns of particular tires. They may even be able to determine the make and model of car to which the tires are usually fitted.

Car tires leave behind tracks that are similar to fingerprints. Each make and model of a tire creates a particular track pattern.

I n most cases, a person's death is not a surprise. People usually die from the effects of old age or as the result of a serious, long-term illness. When a healthy person dies suddenly, murder or suicide may be suspected. If there is any doubt about the cause of death, a pathologist conducts an **autopsy** of the body.

Examination By Autopsy

Autopsy means "seeing for oneself." It is also called post mortem, a **Latin** term that means "after death." In some cases, the cause of death might initially appear obvious, but the pathologist still has to investigate to be sure. A dead person, for example, might appear to have committed suicide by hanging. A pathologist who did not examine the body closely, however, might miss a knife wound that would change a case of suicide to one of murder.

Before a body is placed on an autopsy table, it is weighed and measured, and distinguishing features are noted.

SCIENCE CONCEPTS

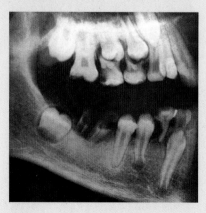

Dental Records

Teeth can be very important for identifying people. Many people pay regular visits to a dentist, and dentists usually keep detailed records of their patients' teeth, often including X rays. In cases of severe fire, teeth may be the only means of identification. An expert who matches dental records to the teeth of an unidentified person is called an odontologist.

Clues from the Body

During an autopsy, a body is laid on an autopsy table and cut open so that every part of it can be examined for injury. To open up the body, the pathologist makes a cut from behind the ear and down to the groin. Any wounds are carefully examined, and foreign objects such as bullets are removed from the body. The pathologist removes internal organs, such as the stomach, intestines, heart, lungs, and brain. These organs are sent out for analysis, which is particularly important if poisoning is suspected. The pathologist also removes the brain for later examination and checks the inside of the skull for old injuries. An experienced pathologist can complete an autopsy in less than an hour.

This facial reconstruction is for the victim of a 1987 fire in London, England. Forensic experts built up a likeness of the victim from a skull discovered in an escalator shaft.

SCIENCE SNAPSHOT

When police find a victim's skeleton or decomposed body, identification can be difficult. Forensic experts, however, can now reconstruct a victim's face from the skull. They use their knowledge to build up the muscles and skin with modeling clay. Then they insert glass eyes, add hair, and paint the face so it looks lifelike. Many unidentified victims have been recognized by relatives or friends using this facial reconstruction.

Skeleton Identification

In many cases of murder, it is difficult to identify the victim, especially if all that remains of the body is a skeleton. Forensic anthropologists study the shape of the skull and pelvis to tell whether the victim is male or female. They can estimate the victim's age, by examining how the bones of the skull have joined together over the years or the condition of the arm and leg bones. An anthropologist can also estimate the height of a victim with only a single arm or leg bone, because the length of such a bone is directly related to a person's height.

Telltale Fluids

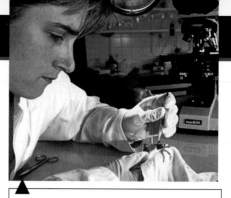

Forensic serology is the study of blood and other bodily fluids for identification purposes following a crime. Forensic serologists are also involved with modern **DNA** profiling techniques, which offer the possibility of identifying people by testing body cells found at a crime scene.

A forensic scientist extracts a sample of blood from a stained cloth for analysis.

Blood Patterns

Forensic investigators often find blood at the scene of a violent crime. If there has been a struggle, both the victim and the attacker may have left behind blood. Scientists study blood splatter patterns to figure out how an attack happened. In the 1930s, the Scottish pathologist John Glauster grouped blood splashes into six distinctive types. Blood that drops vertically will form round spots, and if it falls from a height there will be a "crown" of tiny droplets round the edges. If the victim is struck more than once, there will be a spray of blood from the weapon. This blood will form streaked spots, shaped like exclamation marks, on any nearby surface. If one of the victim's arteries is severed, the pumping action of the heart will send great spurts of blood over a distance, indicating the direction in which the fatal blow was struck. Other traces of blood can show whether the victim's body was moved.

Other Body Fluids

Crime scene investigators may also find other body fluids. They may discover sweat and mucus on a discarded tissue paper or saliva on a cigarette butt or in a bite mark on a victim. Scientists can sometimes tell a person's blood type from saliva, sweat, urine, and other fluids, because 80 percent of people are **secretors** whose blood type can be determined from the fluids they secrete.

SCIENCE CONCEPTS

Clues from Blood

The four basic types of blood are called A, B, AB, and O. Some blood types are more common among people than others, with 42 percent having type A, 8 percent having type B, 47 percent having type O, and only 3 percent having type AB. Forensic investigators often rule out a suspect by comparing the suspect's blood type with the blood types of crime scene samples. Investigators also analyze blood cells to determine if blood found at a crime scene belongs to a man or a woman. Female blood cells have a center called a Barr body, but male blood cells do not.

This machine can test for different blood types.

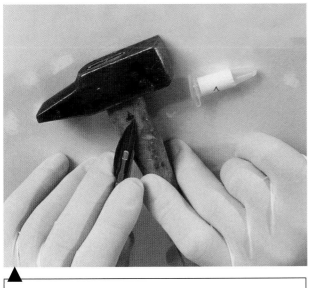

A scientist removes a speck of blood from a murder weapon.

DNA Analysis

All cells of the human body, except for red blood cells, contain DNA. Except for identical twins, no two people have the same DNA. The DNA **molecule** is shaped like a tightly twisted ladder. Forensic scientists analyze short fragments of DNA "ladders" to identify people. If they can match DNA taken from a crime scene with DNA taken from a suspect, they can positively identify that suspect. Alec Jeffreys, a British scientist, invented this "DNA fingerprinting." This analysis takes a long time, but quicker methods have been developed in the United States. These methods use special **enzymes** to multiply a few molecules of DNA into many thousands. This technique is called the polymerase chain reaction, or PCR.

A forensic scientist examines DNA "ladders."

13

Time of Death

In cases of sudden death, particularly if murder is suspected, forensic scientists must work quickly to establish when the person died. Calculating a time of death can confirm or destroy the **alibi** of a murder suspect. Time of death can also be important for insurance claims, or, if a relative has died at about the same time, settling questions about inheritance of money or property.

Looking for clues

The only sure way to know an exact time of death is to be present when the death occurs. Forensic scientists, however, can study a dead body and establish an approximate time of death. The moment a person dies, that person's body begins cooling at a steady rate. By taking the temperature of a dead body, forensic scientists can establish a rough estimate for time of death, to within a few hours. A condition known as **rigor mortis** provides scientists with another way of estimating the time of death. After a person dies, body muscles begin to stiffen. Facial muscles stiffen between one and four hours after death, and limbs stiffen between four and six hours after death. After twelve hours, **bacteria** begin to **decompose** the body's tissues, and the muscles relax.

Entomologists also look at the type of insects found on a corpse to determine when a person died.

Clues from Food

During an autopsy, the pathologist examines the contents of the stomach and small intestine, especially if poisoning is suspected. These organs may contain partially digested food or no food at all. The pathologist will slide the stomach away from other abdominal organs, cut it open, and collect what is inside. A person has to be alive in order to eat. So, if the time of a person's last meal is discovered, investigators will have another rough indication of when the person died.

SCIENCE CONCEPTS

Life Cycles

Forensic entomologists use mathematics to calculate when fly eggs were first laid on a dead body. They know, for example, that one species of maggot will develop to a certain stage in one hundred hours at 50° Fahrenheit (10° Celsius) and fifty hours at 68°F (20°C). Using temperature records for previous days, they calculate a sum called "accumulated degree hours," which enables them to establish, within an hour or two, the time the maggots first emerged.

Insect Invaders

From the moment of a person's death, insects arrive on the body. First to come are blowflies, which lay eggs. In a few hours, the eggs hatch into **larvae**, commonly known as maggots, which begin feeding on the dead flesh. During the next ten to twelve days, the maggots grow. They shed their skins twice, before leaving to become **pupae**, and then emerge as adult flies. Entomologists, or insect biologists, can tell how many days passed since the eggs were laid. Over days, weeks, and months, other insects arrive, in a certain order. These insects can all help indicate when death occurred.

Blowfly larva can appear on a dead body just a few hours after death.

SCIENCE SNAPSHOT

As bacteria gradually decompose a dead body, liquids begin seeping out into the surrounding area. An American scientist named Arpad Vass analyzed the different **compounds** in the liquids and the times at which they appeared. Now, he and his colleagues have developed an electronic "nose," which can detect these compounds and calculate how long a dead body has been lying in the place where it was found.

Measuring the temperature of a dead body helps scientists establish the approximate time of death.

Today, an increasing number of murders are committed with guns. The murderer usually takes the gun from the crime scene, but trace evidence remains. **Shells** from fired bullets may be scattered around the scene, and the bullets themselves may be embedded in the victim. The science of firearm examination is known as ballistics.

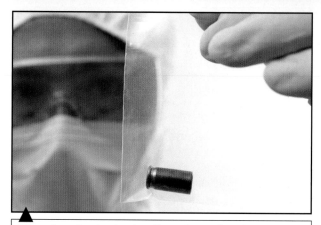

When forensic scientists handle evidence, they always wear protective clothing to prevent contamination.

Looking for the Groove

Almost all firearms are rifled, which means the inside of the barrel has spiral grooves to spin the bullet and make it travel more accurately. These grooves cause marks called striations along the length of the bullet. Every gun manufacturer cuts the grooves in a slightly different way, so the make and model of a firearm is easily determined by examining a bullet fired from it.

Shell Secrets

Shells recovered from a crime scene can also provide important clues about the type of firearm used in the crime. A shell holds an explosive and a bullet. In a gun, the shell lies against a steel **breechblock**. When the gun is fired, a **firing pin** leaves a mark on the base of the shell. The force of the explosion drives the shell back against the breechblock, leaving an impression of any

SCIENCE CONCEPTS

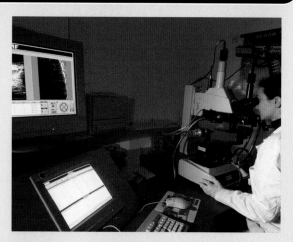

Comparing Bullets

The science of ballistics was established in 1920 by an American named Charles Waite. He spent two years collecting data from gun manufacturers in the United States and Europe. One of Waite's colleagues invented a special microscope, called the comparison microscope, in which two bullets could be laid side by side and the markings on them compared directly.

Laser sights are used to determine the path of a bullet.

imperfections or wear. These marks on a shell can help identify the individual gun used. When investigators recover a weapon they suspect may have been used in a crime, they fire bullets from it. Then, they compare the markings on these bullets with markings on bullets found at the crime scene.

Powder Particles

All guns rely on explosives to fire bullets. When a gun is fired, tiny particles of what remains of the explosive powder are blown back. They can then settle on the hands or clothing of the person who fired the weapon. When people suspected of using a gun in a crime are arrested, their hands are examined. Swabs are used to take samples, which are sent to a laboratory for testing. Scientists analyze the samples for minute traces of **nitrates** from the explosive or use an electron microscope to detect tiny particles of metallic elements, all to prove the suspect fired a gun.

SCIENCE SNAPSHOT

A bullet passing through a human body can change its path dramatically. When U.S. president John F. Kennedy was assassinated, for example, a bullet passed through his head and throat. It then struck Texas governor John Connally and passed through his back and chest. Today, firearms experts use a laser, aligned with the marks found on a victim or at a crime scene, to establish from which direction a bullet was fired and from approximately how far away.

W ords can reveal important clues to forensic investigators. Kidnappers send ransom notes. Other criminals write letters to newspapers or make taunting telephone calls to the police or to the relatives of their victims. Forgers produce fake documents. Unfortunately for criminals, their words are often used to catch them.

Script Secrets

Graphologists can detect a person's characteristics through that person's handwriting. In court, these experts often give evidence that two pieces of writing were written by the same person. This evidence is particularly valuable in cases of kidnapping or forgery. In 1935, for example, Bruno Hauptmann was convicted of the kidnapping and death of famous **aviator** Charles Lindbergh's son,

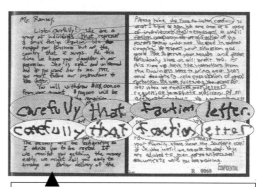

The handwriting examples above show the similarity between Patsy Ramsey's handwriting and the handwriting of the ransom note she found. JonBenet Ramsey is pictured at left.

partially on the evidence of the similarity between his handwriting and that of the ransom note. On December 26, 1996, a six-year-old beauty pageant contestant named JonBenet Ramsey was found murdered in her home. Earlier that morning, Patsy Ramsey, JonBenet's mother, called the authorities to say her daughter had been kidnapped and she had found a ransom note. After studying handwriting samples, the authorities stated that Patsy may have written the note. They could not prove this claim, however, and the case remains unsolved.

SCIENCE CONCEPTS

The Unabomber

For seventeen years, the Federal Bureau of Investigation (FBI) hunted a man who built booby-trap bombs and often sent them in the mail. Known as the "Unabomber," he was responsible for three deaths and twenty-nine serious injuries. In 1995, he sent a 35,000-word "**manifesto**" to two newspapers. A college professor who read the manifesto recognized the writing style of her brother-in-law, Ted Kaczynski. The FBI raided Kaczynski's mountain cabin and found his bomb-making equipment. Kaczynski was sentenced to life imprisonment in 1996.

A Way with Words

The way in which a person uses words, whether in speech or in writing, can also help in identification. One non criminal case is particularly famous. The novel *Primary Colors*, a book many people believe is a thinly disguised portrayal of U.S. president Bill Clinton, was published in 1996 by an author known simply as "Anonymous." A college professor analyzed the text of the novel on his computer and found many unusual words and phrases that identified the author as a well-known journalist. After this success, the FBI consulted the professor in a number of criminal cases. Psychologists can also learn a great deal about the personality of a person from the words and phrases the person uses.

Some scientists use a computerized handwriting recognition system.

SCIENCE SNAPSHOT

When graphologists examine handwriting, they divide the writing into upper, middle, and lower zones and measure the zones' relative sizes. They note if the writing is level or slopes up or down, and they decide if it is bold and confident or thin and scratchy. They also examine the size and importance of individual letters, particularly "t" and "i".

Voice Detectives

When criminals make telephone calls to newspapers, radio stations, or the police, their voices may be recorded. In some cases, criminals have even been interviewed on television with their backs to the cameras. When a suspect is arrested, a recording of the police interview can be compared to other recordings by means of a "voiceprint." Developed in the United States, a voiceprint makes use of an electronic analysis of the sound waves of a voice. A voiceprint can be valuable evidence because no two people's voiceprints are the same. Even professional **mimics** produce voiceprints that differ from the voiceprints of the people they are imitating. Experts can detect age, sex, and race from the sound of a voice. Voiceprints can also reveal slight trembling in a person's voice—a sign the person may be lying.

The most famous fictional detective is Sherlock Holmes. He could tell amazing details about the mind of a criminal from subtle examples of behavior. The person who created Sherlock Holmes, Sir Arthur Conan Doyle, learned the importance of behavior from Dr. Joseph Bell, his teacher in medicine at Scotland's Edinburgh Royal Infirmary. In the last forty years, the FBI has developed its own techniques for studying criminal behavior, known as **psychological profiling**.

The actor Basil Rathbone as Sherlock Holmes, Sir Arthur Conan Doyle's famous detective.

Familiar Methods

Criminals often use the same methods for each crime they commit. This pattern of repeated behavior is known as a **modus operandi**. Called "MO" for short, modus operandi is Latin for "way of working." Some criminals deliberately leave an identifying sign, or "signature," at the scene of a crime. About 1969, the FBI began studying cases of **serial killers**. FBI agents talked to killers who had been caught and sent to prison. The agents began to understand how the minds of killers worked and the ways in which killers typically behaved. Eventually, FBI agents were able to study the evidence of a violent crime and describe the type of person, still unidentified, who had committed the crime and what that person would probably do next. With growing experience, they were able to describe people who had committed other crimes, such as arson or insurance fraud.

SCIENCE CONCEPTS

Crime Classification

In 1992, the FBI published the Crime Classification Manual. Based on records the FBI had gathered, it listed the details of thirty-three types of murder, thirty-five types of arson, and forty-six types of sexual assault. In addition, it established two kinds of serial killers. "Organized" killers choose their victims and often hide the body and clean up the crime scene. "Disorganized" killers pick their victims at random and leave the bodies where they can soon be discovered.

SCIENCE SNAPSHOT

When several crimes are committed in an area, computers can draw a map that pinpoints the probable "base of operation" of the criminal, such as a home district or a social meeting place. This technique, which has been best developed by the Canadian Mounted Police, is known as "geographical profiling."

A woman undergoes an electroencephalograph test, which records electric patterns of the brain.

Telling the Truth

During the 1930s, law enforcement authorities hoped the **polygraph**, or "lie detector," would show when a suspect lied during questioning. The machine failed so many times, however, that today it is rarely used. The polygraph's modern equivalent is a machine called the **electroencephelograph** (ECG). This machine scans the electrical waves that pass through the brain. It detects changes in brain waves that might occur when a guilty person hears particular phrases or is shown evidence from a crime. Use of this machine is known as "brain fingerprinting." In one case, a man who is on **death row** in Oklahoma has asked to be given an ECG test to prove he is innocent of the murders for which he was sentenced to death.

Global Police Force

In 1985, the FBI began to keep a computer record of all violent crimes. With this information, FBI agents were able to compare murders committed over a wide area and decide if the same killer was responsible for all the murders. Today, the FBI trains police officers from all over the world in the skills of psychological profiling. The use of psychological profiling has led to the capture of many criminals in the United States and in other countries.

A policeman marks a map with sites of shootings during the hunt for a sniper in the Washington, D.C., area in 2003.

Forensic laboratories usually keep extensive records, together with a wide range of samples, of most manufactured products. These products may include many kinds of paint, glass, paper and synthetic fibers, and clothing. When a plane exploded above the tiny Scottish town of Lockerbie in 1988, forensic investigators were able to draw on an extensive database to track down the culprits.

Disaster from the Sky

When a PanAm 747 called *Maid of the Sea* exploded over Lockerbie, Scotland, on December 21, 1988, all 259 persons aboard the plane died. Huge pieces of the aircraft fell upon Lockerbie, killing another 11 people and destroying a number of houses. Smaller pieces of the plane were scattered over an area of 845 square miles (2,190 square kilometers). Some pieces were carried 45 miles (72 km) away by a strong westerly wind. Searchers eventually recovered about four million fragments, which were laid out at the Army Central Ammunition Depot, near Lockerbie, for examination. The searchers found pieces of a luggage container and fragments of a brown suitcase that had been inside it. The suitcase had held the bomb. An accident inspector also found a tiny piece of printed circuit board, identified as part of a Toshiba radio-cassette player.

Forensic scientists investigate the shattered nose of the plane used for Pan Am Flight 903 (top) and examine fragments (right) that had been scattered across the Scottish town of Lockerbie.

Piecing Together the Clues

Researchers at the Royal Armament Research & Development Establishment (RARDE), in Fort Halsted, Kent, England, found more fragments of the Toshiba player and calculated that it had been packed with about 14 ounces (397 grams) of **Semtex** explosive. Later, they found a fragment of an electronic timer that had been used to produce the explosion. Only twenty examples of this particular timer had been manufactured, in Switzerland, and they had been sold to the government of Libya. More searches of the wreckage turned up fragments of clothing, including a label that read "Malta Trading Company."

A Trail to Libya

Police inquiries in Malta led to the discovery of the trader who had sold the clothing, and he was able to describe the Libyan man who had bought it. Three years later, U.S. and Scottish authorities named two Libyan men as being responsible for the bomb. In 1999, the two men were finally brought to trial, at a special court in the Netherlands. In January 2001, only one was found guilty, and there are still questions about the verdict. Nevertheless, in August 2003, Libya's leader, Colonel Muammar al-Qaddafi, announced that $2.7 billion in compensation would be paid to relatives of the Lockerbie bombing victims.

Commemorative tombstones list the names of the people who died from the Lockerbie bombing.

Case Study: the Fate of the Romanovs

E ven when a body has completely decomposed, the bones left behind still provide a wealth of forensic evidence. Anthropologists are able to identify the age and sex of the person and calculate height. When faced with a jumble of bones from several different people, they can still sort them out. The latest analytical methods also make it possible to extract DNA from the bones. Several forensic techniques were used to help solve the riddle of the Romanovs.

Death of the Russian Royal Family

After the Russian Revolution of 1917, the Romanov royal family—**Tsar** Nicholas II, his wife, and their five children—were imprisoned in a house in Siberia. On July 16, 1918, the Romanov family, along with their doctor and servants, were executed by firing squad. Six months later, Russian investigator Nicholas Sokolov announced that the bodies had been thrown in a mine shaft, soaked in **sulphuric acid**, and consumed by fire.

New Clues

In 1989, filmmaker Gely Ryabov announced that he had found bones and scraps of clothing at a site 5 miles (8 km) from the mine shaft. In 1991, Russian president Boris Yeltsin gave permission for the site to be **excavated**. About one thousand pieces of bone and skulls were unearthed and assembled into four male and five female skeletons. Russian scientists examined the skulls. The scientists decided two were missing, those of the Tsar's son, Alexei, and daughter, Marie.

Tsar Nicholas II and his family, shortly before they were executed

24

A 1956 film starring Ingrid Bergman (right) told the story of Anastasia, a Romanov family member whom some people believed had escaped execution.

Solving the Mystery?

A Russian DNA expert took the remains to England, where he analyzed them with a scientist from the British Forensic Science Service. They found that five skeletons were related. The Tsar's wife was identified with a DNA sample provided by her grandnephew, the Duke of Edinburgh. To prove the identity of the Tsar, his brother's tomb was opened. DNA analysis of both skeletons proved they were related.

A Final Twist

Questions about the bones persisted. Only nine skeletons had been found, but eleven people were believed to have been executed. A team of American experts had suggested that one of the missing skulls belonged to another daughter, Anastasia. For many years, it had been rumored that Alexei and Anastasia had escaped execution. A woman named Anna Anderson had claimed all her life that she was Anastasia. An American hospital had kept a sample of her tissue after an operation. In 1994, thirty years after her death, DNA analysis of this tissue proved that Anna Anderson was actually a Polish woman named Franzisca Schanzkowska. Members of the Schanzkowska family provided DNA samples to prove this fact.

> "From the very start of my involvement in the case it was clear to me Anna Anderson was Schanzkowska."
> —Dr. Von Berenberg-Gossler, an attorney who had long opposed Anderson's claim that she was Anastasia

Case Study Fact File

- The Romanovs, the Russian royal family, were executed by Russian communists on July 16, 1918.
- Authorities in the Soviet Union tried to cover up the execution of the Romanovs for more than seventy years.
- The location of the bodies was a mystery until 1989, when the possible remains of the Romanovs were discovered in Russia.
- Living relatives of the Romanovs, including Prince Philip of Great Britain, gave blood for DNA testing to determine if the remains were of the Romanovs.
- In 2004, scientists from Stanford University questioned the DNA test results because of the way samples were collected.

Forensic scientists concluded that these remains were of the Romanov family.

Case Study: the Death of Captain Hall

For hundreds of years, poisoning was a common form of murder. Investigating cases of poison was difficult, partly because there was often no way to establish the specific poison used. In the nineteenth century, however, the scientific study of poison, called toxicology, was founded. Toxicologists have helped to solve many murders, including the murder of the explorer Charles Francis Hall.

Dr. Emil Bessels, the chief scientist on board the Polaris.

Death of a Hero

In 1871, Charles Francis Hall led an American expedition into the Arctic in search of the North Pole. Traveling on a steamship, the *Polaris*, the expedition reached a point on the north coast of Greenland, about 500 miles (800 km) from the Pole. Hall decided to spend the winter at this place, naming it Thank God Harbor. From the beginning of the voyage, Hall had quarreled with his chief scientist, a German named Dr. Emil Bessels. One evening Hall drank a cup of coffee, and he soon became violently sick. He stayed in bed, where Dr. Bessels treated him. Hall gradually grew worse, and two weeks later, he died and was buried on shore. His crew suspected that he had been poisoned, but the truth was not known for almost a century.

The Mystery Solved

In 1968, two scientists flew to Thank God Harbor and dug up Hall's body. They took samples of hair and fingernails, which were analyzed at the Toronto Center of Forensic Sciences in Canada. Scientists used a modern technique called **neutron activation analysis**. They found enough arsenic in Hall's fingernails to indicate that he had received a huge dose during the last two weeks of his life.

Today, forensic scientists can easily detect the presence of poisons such as arsenic.

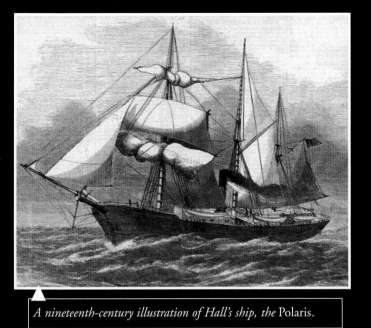

A nineteenth-century illustration of Hall's ship, the Polaris.

Early Poisoners

In the nineteenth century, arsenic was the most common poison used by murderers. Arsenic is a white powder, with a faint, sweet taste that is easily disguised by foods with strong flavors. People who are poisoned with arsenic become very sick. In the past, doctors often mistakenly decided that arsenic victims had died from **gastric** disease. Arsenic was widely used as a rat poison. It was sold at pharmacies and other stores and was even sold to young children. In the 1830s, an English **chemist** named James Marsh devised a way to test for very small amounts of arsenic in the body. This test was used successfully in a famous murder case in France. After this case, many countries passed laws controlling the sale of arsenic.

* The *Polaris* left New London, Connecticut, on July 3, 1871, bound for the Arctic.
* The ship had enough supplies on board to support the crew of thirty-three men for up to two years.
* After Hall's death, the *Polaris* remained trapped in ice for ten months.
* When the *Polaris* returned to the United States, authorities questioned the crew and decided that Hall died of natural causes.
* The first accurate analytical test for arsenic is known as the Marsh test and is named after James Marsh, the chemist who developed it.
* The chemical name for arsenic is arsenious oxide.

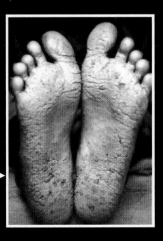

Scientists now know that arsenic poisoning can turn skin to a green color.

27

Proving that a document is a forgery can be very difficult. In order to conduct a chemical analysis of a document's ink or paper, a piece of the document must be destroyed. **Carbon dating** also requires a small sample. These methods can be helpful, but sometimes what is needed is a sharp eye for a telltale clue. It was just such a clue that led to the eventual capture of the **Mormon** bomber Mark Hofmann.

Professional Forger

Mark Hofmann lived in Salt Lake City, Utah, where he made a nice profit forging rare documents and selling them to the Mormon Church. In 1985, he offered a single sheet of paper to the **Library of Congress**, at a price of one million dollars. This paper was "The Oath of a Freeman," printed in 1639, and no example was known to have survived. Photocopies of another work from the same medieval printer, the *Bay Psalm Book*, were easily available, and Hofmann based his forgery of the "The Oath of a Freeman" on these photocopies. He used a blank piece of paper from an old book and made ink by burning the leather binding of another old book, so that carbon-dating would confirm that his document was old. Then he had a printing plate made from his pasted-up text. At first, experts could not decide if the Oath was genuine. Then a document examiner at the Arizona State Crime Laboratory reported that, out of seventy-nine documents Hofmann had sold to the Mormon Church, twenty-one were probably forgeries.

One of Hofmann's bombs actually went off in his car.

> "All along, of course, until the evening that I made them, I didn't really think that I would end up using them. At least to take a life."
>
> —Mark Hofmann, on making bombs

A fake letter that Mark Hofmann sold to the Mormon Church

From Forgery to Murder

To draw attention away from the investigation into his documents, Hofmann decided to send bombs to several top members of the church. On November 15, 1985, Hofmann planted a bomb that killed a document collector, Steven Christensen. Later that day, another bomb planted by Hofmann killed Kathy Sheets, the wife of Christensen's employer. Hofmann created a third bomb, but it went off in his car, injuring him badly and arousing the suspicion of the police. In the end, however, it was a county attorney who brought Hofmann to justice. The attorney had spent seventeen years in the printing industry and knew all about **type**. He showed how Hofmann had made photographs of the *Bay Psalm Book*, cut out letters he needed, and pasted them together to make the text of his forgery. Many of the letters, however, were closer together than they should have been if set in type. Hofmann was arrested for murder and forgery. In 1987, he pled guilty to lesser, related charges to avoid the death penalty and was sentenced to life in prison.

The forger and murderer Mark Hofmann was sent to prison for life in 1987.

Case Study Fact File

• Mark Hofmann spent two years as a Mormon missionary, but he developed great doubts about the Mormon Church's account of its origins.

• After his missionary work, Hofmann became a dealer in antique documents.

• Many of the Mormon documents Hofmann claimed to have found were very critical of the church. The "Salamander Letter," for example, claimed that a founding figure practiced folk magic.

• Hofmann's lack of knowledge of typography techniques eventually led to him being caught.

29

Glossary

acquitted: found not guilty of a crime.

algae: microscopic, plantlike organisms.

alibi: from the Latin word for "elsewhere," proof that a person was not near a crime scene at the time the crime was committed.

anthropologists: scientists who study the characteristics and cultures of human beings.

arson: the crime of deliberately setting a fire.

autopsy: the detailed examination of a dead body to determine the cause of death or study the effects of disease.

aviator: a person who flies aircraft.

bacteria: a large group of single-celled, microscopic organisms, some of which turn dead organisms and organic waste into substances that can be used by plants.

ballistics: the study of the path that a projectile, such as a bullet, takes. Ballistics now commonly refers to the technical examination of bullets and firearms involved in crimes.

biologists: scientists who study living things.

breechblock: the part of a gun that keeps explosive gases from escaping.

burglary: breaking into a home or other building to commit a crime, such as theft.

carbon dating: a method for determining the age of an object by measuring the level of carbon in it.

chemist: a scientist who studies what things are made of and how they change.

communists: people who believe that a country's government should own all or most property and should control the country's economy.

compounds: combinations of substances.

contamination: in forensics, the introduction of outside substances to a sealed crime scene.

death row: the area in a prison where people sentenced to death are housed.

decompose: break down after death. A human body will begin to break down soon after death, as bacteria digest the internal organs of the body and gradually spread to the exterior.

defense: in a court of law, the lawyer or lawyers who defend a person charged with a crime.

DNA: the abbreviation for deoxyribonucleic acid, the chemical in cells that determines the characteristics of organisms. Except for identical twins, no two people have the same DNA, but people who are related have similar DNA.

electroencephalograph: a device that detects the electrical activity of the brain and displays that activity as waves on a video screen.

entomology: the scientific study of insects.

enzymes: substances produced by a living thing that set off chemical reactions.

excavated: dug a hole or dug around something to expose or remove it.

extortion: the crime of forcing a person to provide something, such as money, by using physical harm or some other threat.

firing pin: the part of a gun that strikes the end of a bullet when the trigger is pulled, causing the explosive charge in the bullet's shell to ignite.

forensic pathology: a branch of medicine having to do with examining bodies to find evidence of a crime.

fraud: the crime of deceiving a person to get something of value, such as money or property.

gastric: having to do with the digestive system.

graphologists: people who study handwriting.

larvae: insects in their early, wormlike form.

Latin: a language, originally created by Romans thousands of years ago, that is the basis for English and other modern languages.

Library of Congress: the national library of the United States, based in Washington, D.C.

magistrate: a government official, often a judge.

manifesto: a document that publicly expresses the author's views or plans.

medical examiner: a person who investigates cases of murder or suspicious death by examining the victim's body and the crime scene. Medical examiners also testify in court about what they discover in their investigations.

mimics: people who can imitate other people.

modus operandi: the characteristic way in which a criminal commits crimes.

molecule: a combination of atoms that makes up a specific chemical compound.

Mormon: a follower of Mormonism or having to do with Mormonism, a world religion founded by Joseph Smith in the United States in 1830. Mormonism is a Christian religion, but it differs from other Christian faiths in many ways.

neutron activation analysis: a method used to identify extremely small traces of elements.

nitrates: chemical compounds that provide the oxygen necessary to set off an explosive.

polygraph: the name for a collection of devices that record changes in a person's body, which might indicate the person is lying.

pupae: insects in the stage of their life cycle when they are changing into adults.

psychological profiling: the method of establishing the probable personalities and future behavior of criminals, based on the study of their crimes.

psychologists: people who study the human mind and human behavior.

rigor mortis: the stiffening of a body's muscles that begins soon after death.

samples: in forensics, small quantities of material collected for comparison or other examination.

secretors: people whose blood type can be determined from body fluids, such as saliva.

Semtex: one of the most powerful plastic explosives in the world, manufactured in the Czech Republic.

serial killers: criminals who have murdered three or more people, with an interval of time between each murder.

serologists: people who study body fluids.

shells: the outer casings of bullets, which contain the explosive powder that propels the bullets. Most modern guns eject shells after firing.

Soviet Union: a former communist nation, consisting of Russia and other neighboring republics, that was established in 1922 and broke apart in 1991.

sulphuric acid: a chemical that can quickly destroy human tissue.

toxicologists: scientists who analyze poisons and understand their effects upon the human body.

trace: a tiny piece of physical evidence.

tsar: before 1917, the king of Russia.

type: in a printing press, a piece of metal that has an impression of a particular letter and makes an imprint of the letter, in ink, on a page.